Memories Have Tongue

POETRY BY

Afua Cooper

Sister Vision
Black Women and Women of Colour Press

ISBN 0-920813-50-X

Cover: *Rio Bueno, Trelawney, Jamaica.*
Production & design: *Stephanie Martin*
Printed and bound in Canada by union labour

The author wishes to thank the Ontario Arts Council, the Toronto Arts Council and the Secretary of State (Multiculturalism) for its financial assistance during the writing of this book.

Canadian Cataloguing in Publication Data
Cooper, Afua.
        Memories Have Tongue
Poems.
ISBN 0-920813-50-X
I. Title.
PS8555.066M4 1992   C811'.54   C92-093853-1
PR9199.3.C66M4 1992

Published by:
        SISTER VISION
        Black Women and Women of Colour Press
        P.O. Box 217
        Station E
        Toronto, Ontario
        Canada M6H 4E2

Published with the assistance of the Canada Council and the Ontario Arts Council

In Memory of my three grandmothers:
Rachel, Georgiana and Christina.

Preface

These poems were written over a six year period, from
1985-1991. The manuscript was partially completed at the
Banff school of Fine Arts in the spring of 1988. Final completion occurred in 1990-91. Between the starting and completion
of this manuscript I completed a master's degree and started
a Ph.D.

These poems came out of my experiences of being a woman,
a mother, a black person, an immigrant, a student, a daughter,
a grand-daughter, a lover and a wife. There are also several
settings for these poems: rural and urban Jamaica, Toronto
and North America and also importantly the interior spaces of
one woman, the poet.

This collection seeks to bridge the inner and the outer
worlds, the private and the public. It seeks a comprimise. The
poems are saying that one needs a public and political life but
that also the inner life is of vital importance: in order to
preserve one's sanity in a hostile world one has to sometimes
seek the solace of inner spaces.

What exactly is an inner space? Carl Jung and others
who have spent their lifetime studying the human psychology,
speak of the unconscious and that getting to know one's
unconscious is getting to know one's self more intimately. One
becomes intimate with one's unconscious by paying attention
to one's dreams, by practising meditation, by engaging in
prayer. As this manuscript was being produced I started a
dialogue with my unconscious and I received valuable gifts.
The poem, "the Black Madonna" is one of the many poetic gifts
received from the unconscious. Sometimes this dialogue is
precipitated by crises in one's life and I have had my share of
personal crises as this mauscript was being produced. Several

poems reflect the state of crisis. But crises, if seen as lessons, can lead to self-knowledge. Interior reflections are necessary for wholistic growth but so is political awareness. For all my years in Canada (and even before) I have lead an active political/public life fighting a racist patriarchal structure.

One other thing that emerged from political life was that I realised that for many people (and they have the right) an inner life, or a religious life if you will, was not of importance. In fact anything that smacked of contemplativeness was derided. Of course, many of us that came from the Judeo-Christian traditions rejected Christianity at an early age for reasons we all know, but in doing so, we often shut ourselves off from rich inner experiences. If we look at the poetic works of some of our Caribbean and American poet-sisters like Olive Senior and Audre Lorde we find that the theme of the inner space runs through them. These poets know that after fighting the partriarchy without and within, they have to have somewhere to retreat, to think, to grow strong again.

As I wrote this manuscript, myths from the Judeo/Christian/Islamic traditions visited me. Bible stories from my childhood days became vivid. Pithy Rastafari sayings came to fore and the myths from the prophetic traditions took on new meanings. But also importantly, ancient religious symbology burst on the screen of my mind. These were mainly women's religious myths, Isis and Demeter to name a few. And you can image my joy and surprise when I discovered the Great Mother, the female deity of the Caribbean Arawaks (one of the Natives people of the region), Atabeyra. Although the Antillean Caribbean Arawaks were exterminated by the Spaniards, I believe their mythologies went underground and later resurfaced in the dreams and artistic work of the present people inhabiting their islands.

Recovering the culture and myths of these Aboriginal people is also part of finding and knowing my own story. Several of these ancient universal myths guided and underlined my work making it distinctly female. Even in the decidedly male prophetic traditions I found the submerged female principle; and though submerged she is still pivotal. For example, Hagar in all fairness can be called "The Mother of Islam." Because of her the city of Mecca was established and her son was the progenitor of Prophet Muhammad. She is one of the many dark women with "numen" whose sons became prophets.

As can be seen, my childhood profoundly affected my writing. In those early days in Westmoreland I felt secured and loved. I grew up in a village where I was related to by almost everyone and that gave me confidence and security. Apart from my parents, my paternal grandmother was the most pivotal person in my early life. She was my best friend. She was also my teacher and through her I came to learn of my story and the myths that informed it. She was the one who started me on the journey of stepping into the ancestors' shoes. From her I received my love of herstory and history. From her I received my love of language and the written word. Yes, this manuscript is also about ancestors. Without the ancestors this work would not have been possible because they are balancing me on their shoulders.

The experiences of the immigrant also come to fore. We see her as the other, the stranger, the unwanted.

It is through my student's exeriences that I came upon the reality of American slave women escaping to Canada and also discovering that Canadians too kept slaves. One of them, Marie Joseph Angélique set fire to Montréal. Though my studies at the Academe have been often arduous and alienat-

ing I have found many Black women like Angélique beckoning
me from the lost pages of herstory.

As is obvious by now the figure of the feminine, especially
that of the mother has been very influential in my life. The
figure has been nourishing and beneficent but she has also
been negative. We are reminded of the earth which is at once
the nourisher and the destroyer.

The poems about aunts reflect well the double-faced mother.
Anger and rage also spill from these pages.

Daily mediating my life, in a society where I am con-
fronted by racism, the pen is sometimes used as my weapon
and so "Dancing on Skulls," "My Piece," and "Founding Peoples" are well aimed arrows.

This collection is also about healing. The broken hearted
must be soothed, the wounds must heal and the tears must be
dried. We know that weeping endureth for the night, but joy
cometh in the morning. A redemptive joy. As I journey on the
way back home to myself forgiveness also becomes easier.
This collection is also about charting my course, finding my
story and to be able to live it and tell it. It is in this process that
I am presently engaged. I hope to succeed.

With much love,
A.C

*p.s. This collection is about many things I have not mentioned.
Read it!*

CONTENTS

THE LEARNING TREE II

DANCING ON SKULLS

CELEBRATIONS

Acknowledgements

To the women at Sister Vision Press, a special thanks for support and editorial advice. To Sylmadel Coke, Alpha Diallo, Sharon Fernandez, Gayap Rhythm Drummers, Jim Hodgins, Ahdri Zhina Mandiela, Marlene Nourbese Philip, Akil Powell, Audrey Rose, Hamid Shaqq, John Smith (University of Prince Edward Island), Patrick Andrade and to all who supported me one way or the other in my literary endeavors, thanks.

MEMORIES HAVE TONGUE I

Sing me my history O earth mother
about tongues multiplying memories...
SONIA SANCHEZ

How you call to me, call to me
Voices in sleep
Echoes of storms stilled, dusks, dawns ago
Before my own instant furled
Out of the turning world.

JEAN D'COSTA

My ancestors are nearer
than albums of pictures
I tread on heels thrust
into broken-down slippers

OLIVE SENIOR

And I Remember

And I remember
standing
in the churchyard on Wesleyan hill
standing and looking down on the plains
that stretched before me
like a wide green carpet
the plains full with sugar cane and rice
the plains that lead to the sea

And I remember
walking
as a little girl to school
on the savannas of Westmoreland
walking from our hillbound village
along steep hillsides
walking carefully so as not to trip and plunge
walking into the valley

And I remember
running
to school on the road that cuts into the green carpet
running past laughing waters
running past miles of sugar cane and paddies of rice
running to school that rose like a concrete castle
running with a golden Westmoreland breeze

And I remember
breathing
the smell of the earth plowed by rain and tractors
breathing the scent of freshly cut cane

15

breathing the scent of rice plants as they send
their roots into the soft mud

and I remember
thinking
this is mine   this is mine
this sweetness of mountains
valleys
rivers
and plains
is mine
mine
mine

On the Way to Sunday School

And running wildly up the road with Jean and Doris
stoning Mass Brutus dog
stealing Miss Clarice mangoes
laughing raucously as Doris tells the latest dirty joke
the river, the river
we cannot resist
not on this sun morning
so off comes our shoes
we are about to wade in when
a shadow falls upon us/we look up/to behold
sister Iris stiff and white in her holiness

My Father's Mother

My father's mother was a tall woman
who never showed her age
who in our childhood was our best friend
when we felt sad we visited
when our parents threatened
we escaped to her warm hearth
she brewed chocolate, made fried dumplings and saltfish
sat in the yard with us and told
stories about the strikes and riots
the birth of my sister in the 1951 storm
about one of her uncles who went
to help build the Panama canal and never came back
of her husband who died
so young
my grandmother always left dinner for us
so at eveningtime we had two meals
and she never went shopping without buying
something for us
my father's mother indulged us so much
that when our parents thought we were uncontrollable
they'd attribute it to her

Memories Have Tongue

My granny say she have a bad memory
when I ask her to tell
me some of her life
say she can't remember much but
she did remember the 1910 storm and how
dem house blow down
an dey had to go live with her granny
down bottom house.

Say she have a bad memory, but she remember
that when her husband died, both of them were thirty,
she had three little children, one in her womb,
one in her arms, one at her frocktail.
She remember when
they bury him how the earth buss up under her foot
and her heart bruk inside
that when the baby born she had no milk
her breasts refused to yield.

She remember how she wanted
her daughter to grow up and be
a post-mistress but the daughter died at an early age
she point to the croton-covered grave at the bottom
of the yard. Say her memory bad, but she remember
1938
Frome
the riot
Busta
Manley

but what she memba most of all is that a
pregnant woman,
one of the protesters, was shot and killed by soldiers.

Say she old now   her brains gathering water
but she remember
that she liked dancing as a young woman
and yellow was her favourite colour.
she remember too
that it was her husband's father who asked
for her hand. The parents sat in the hall and discussed
the matter. Her father concluded that her man
was an honourable person and so gave his consent.

Her memory bad but she remember
on her wedding day how some of her relatives
nearly eat off all the food.
It was alright though, she said,
I was too nervous to eat anyway.

Song of Willie

Willie went a-courtin in his Panama suit
there were three girls
and he didn't know which one he wanted
but he knew he wanted one
so he went a-courtin in his Panama suit
and his knowledge of the world

but Willie wasn't tall you know
wasn't handsome either
was short, bow-legged
but was a good dresser

The youngest girl was Adiana
and she said yes but he had to ask her father
when the father heard he nodded his head
so Willie and Addie went to the marriage bed

Four children they had
one after the other
four children who were told tales of bandits
of a land where potatoes are the size of pumpkins
of a land where the people speak a strange language
to his wife he told stories of Black workers
who were treated worse than animals

Willie went to work at the Sugar estate
they made him headman, a terrible fate
for at 33, his stomach start to ache
ache so bad he could not stand up

they took him to the doctor
his skin had gotten blacker
let him make peace with his maker

he died, oh he died
in his 33rd year
leaving four young children
and a still young wife

At the funeral the pastor said
Willie was a good father
a very good provider
he was our son and we miss him so

and Addie she cried, oh how she cried
they had to hold her up
lest she fall to the ground
and in her grief she remembered
that day in November
when her Willie came a-courtin in his Panama suit

Roots and Branches

Robbing peoples and countries of their rightful names was one of the cruel games that colonizers played with the colonized. Names are like magic markers in the long and labyrinthine streams of racial memory, for racial memories are rivers leading to the sea where the memory of mankind [sic] is stored. To rob people or countries of their name is to set in motion a psychic disturbance that can, in turn, create a permanent crisis of identity.

JAN CAREW

I cannot possibly say to you that I am a woman descendent from the people of the Plains - the Serengeti, of Kenya, of Ghana, of Gambia or of Zaire - the heartland. I can only look to the vast expanse of Africa, that black mother continent, and say, that is who and what and where I am.

MAXINE TYNES

Which one of you was a teacher
which one of you was a healer
a warrior
a merchant
a weaver
a diplomat
which one tilled the soil

Which one was from Dahomey
the Congo
SeneGambia
Angola
The Gold Coast
which one was Hausa

Fula
Igbo
Mande
which one?

I hear that Congo Nancy
my grandfather's mother was black as coal and she was
a fighter
a warrior woman
who used her forehead as her weapon
yes, she was Nanny's daughter herself

And Neil her son
my mother's father
Neil the sugar boiler
was tall, handsome and thin
and the women would go crazy for him
he was a master sugar boiler
as he made large quantities of sugar
from small amounts of cane

and his wife
grandma Rachel
was a gentle woman
a four eye woman who saw things before they happened
she was a herbalist who healed and cured many
and yes, she had the best voice in the Methodist choir
steal away, steal away, steal away to Jesus
steal away, steal away Oh
I am not to stay here
My mother tells me that her mama's mama

greatgrandma Yodi grew
the biggest yams for miles around
but to her ill-luck, for she was envied and obeahed
and as a result lost one of her legs
but she was undaunted
for she began to make asham and sold it to people
from her doorsteps

And Tata
my father's maternal grandfather
Tata the old African
who insisted on riding his horse everywhere he went
he married a woman of considerable height
my great grandma Mimi

And Willie Cooper, my other grandpa
grew the best roses in the neighbourhood
went to work in Panama
and became an instant celebrity
upon his return to Jamaica
his prestige increased when he took
my grandma and their children
for a brief sojourn in Cuba

And of the others, the others that came before
I do not know much
I only know that they too lived in the western county
and tilled the soil
at dusktime they'd sit on their doorsteps
smoked their pipes whilst protected by
the blue mountains of Westmoreland

My Mother

My mother planted fields
married a man
bore ten children
and still found time
to run her own business
I remember once
She and I
were going to work
the plot of land
she rented from someone
we heard the missionary's car
coming down the road
she jumped over a culvert to hide
because she had on a pair
of my father's pants
the church disapproved of women
wearing men's clothing
when the sun was steadily going westward
we hurried from the field
she had to rush home
to cook the family's meal
she seemed able to do anything
and I think that in one
of her past lives
she was a leader of some sort

my mother planted fields
married a man
bore ten children
and still found time
to run her own business.

Christopher Columbus

With the unification of Castile and Aragon
Spain became one nation
Under the rule of Isabel and Ferdinand
Columbus sailed to this little island

what did he come for
he came for gold
what did he bring
miseries untold

The statue of Columbus stands on the hill facing the sea
his hand rests on the hilt on his sword
I walk beneath the statue
his feet crush my brain
his sword cuts open my womb
I flee, I flee from beneath his shadow
my blood dripping to the ground

As a little girl in grade four
the teacher would take us to see
this statue and we would attempt to draw-etch-
this conqueror of new lands
we were made to repeat
(and every schoolchild knows this)
"Christopher Columbus discovered Jamaica in 1494
with his three ships,
the Nina
Pinta
and Santa Maria

I look at the statue
its shadow covers the sun
and all around me are graves and spirits of
a vanquished people

I look again at the statue
remembering the grade four chant
remembering a beautiful land
remember death and tears
I look again at the statue
and marvel that even today
we still honour our conquerors.

500 Years of Discovery

I am still trying to understand my place in this place called the Americas. Still trying to understand my place in this new world, in this hemisphere. I'm still trying to understand my relationship with this land. I, island woman, Black African Jamaican woman whose ancestry sprang from another continent, another hemisphere, am still trying to understand my place in these Americas.

These American continents in recent histories have had a history of blood. In my home island hundreds of thousands of Arawak Indians were massacred by the Spaniards who came thirsty, seeking gold. The same fate befell the Arawaks from other islands. The Arawaks were described as a peaceful people loving art and music, they were not prepared for the barbarity of the Spaniards. The Carib Indians, on the other hand, were described as warlike; they survived. They mounted a strong resistance against the Spaniards and to this day have descendants in the smaller islands of the West Indies. Is there a lesson to be learned from this, that it is those who are 'warlike' who survived?

In my home island, what was left of the blood of the Arawaks was mixed in with that of African slaves who fled to the mountains on the conquest of the British, to become the first Maroons. I think of how the Spanish killed the Arawaks of Jamaica and replaced their labour with that of African slaves, the labour of my foreparents who have given their freedom, blood, sweat and tears for the island.

How can I mourn for the Arawaks? The only remnants of them are in a museum at White Marl in Spanish Town. The curator has dutifully shown on a map the location of Arawak villages throughout the island. The town where I once lived,

Seville (Sevilla Nueva) was one such village. The curator also tells how at White Marl, mass graves were found as if a massacre or mass suicide had taken place.

But we know the means by which the Indians were killed by the Spaniards:
European diseases
mass slaughter
forced labour and slavery
suicide
infanticide.

Mothers preferred to kill their young rather than see them end up as slaves or sport things of the Spanish. Oppression is worse than death.[1]

I believe the spirits of the Arawaks cry out to be expressed. To be frozen in museums, on coats of arms or on national money is not enough. How will their history be written? And when will we mourn. Because mourning is necessary. Thousands of people were wiped from a small island in the West Indies. This has to be acknowledged as a brutal crime. Instead, what we have today is the descendants of those who unleashed this holocaust on the Indians, preparing a celebration in order to remember their criminal ancestor(s). But for the spiritual and physical descendants of the Arawaks, this is not a matter of celebration but of recovery, remembering and rejoicing in our survival.

I think of the Aztec in the valley of Mexico, of Moctezuma, and again of the mass murders that the Spanish carried out against these people. The fate of the Aztecs was repeated in South America, Peru, Ecuador, Chile. The Incas. The name Pizarro is synonymous with the destruction of Incan civilization. All over Central and South American the same story was enacted as men of iron came with their greedy ambitions.

Fleeing a medieval Europe that had gone sour.

And today in some places the extermination of aboriginal peoples is still being carried out. Look at Brazil and the Indians in the Amazon: cattle ranching, McDonalds, multinationals.

I think of the continent on which I presently live. Called Turtle Island by the First Nations Peoples of this land, called North America by Europeans. I live in the northern half of this continent—Canada. This Turtle Island too has suffered a similar fate as her sister continents. We know how the spanish, dutch, french and english tricked the Indians of their land, took it by brutal warfare and engaged in mass murders as they did in the southern continents. Biological warfare was also carried out on the First Peoples of this land. Remember infested blankets. Many cultures were destroyed. The wonderful plains culture of the Sioux, the woman-oriented civilisation of the Iroquois, the Behoteks of Newfoundland, and countless others.

How shall we mourn the tragedy that befell these lands? How shall we mourn the shedding of blood? How shall we mourn the loss of millions of lives? How shall we mourn the destruction of a people's culture? The tales of woe are too much to hear, to bear, to be written down; but they must be made known. And we must find appropriate ways to mourn; it is the only way we can begin to heal.

The nations of Europe have all come to these continents to suck the blood of the land and the people, they all came to feast; to drink blood. They, of no human heart.

When the natives of the islands and the mainlands were subdued and their labour not of use the Spaniards brought in African slaves. Bartholomew Las Casas, his conscience twinged. "Let the African take their place," he said and a new wave of exploitation began. The European slave trade.

When the story of the African in the new world is being told it often begins with slavery, but Africans arrived here centuries before Columbus. They came from the kingdom of Mali, from ancient Egypt, from Moorish Spain. In the Yucatan, on Turtle Island, in Peru these Africans lived among the native inhabitants. Africans with their advanced navigational technology were already visiting these parts of the world before Columbus and making friendly contacts with the people here. They came not as slaves but as free people, curious, generous and world travelled. No doubt African/Indian relations were established then.

At a later date in the 17th century in Acadia, Canada, an African who served as a Micmac interpreter married a Micmac woman. His name is Matthieu D'Coste. Their descendants still abound. We know stories of African slaves in the United States escaping bondage to live among Indians. They became known as Black Indians. After the pacification of Turtle Island when many First Nations people were designated into bands many obvious looking Blacks were among them who identified themselves as being of particular Indian nations.

I am still defining my relations with this land, these continents, this hemisphere. That I am treading on land not originally mine is true. But my forebears have lived here for centuries and have given their lives and their freedom. Those who came as slaves, came against their will. The cost they paid in being dragged here was/is too much: millions died in the middle passage, millions died in the holds of ships, millions died in slave forts and castles, millions died on plantations, farms and mines. We did not want to come here, we were the unwilling migrants. Our pain and tragedy followed closely on that of the destruction of the first peoples of these lands. Yet it is the labour of the Indians and Africans and the exploitation of both by the Europeans that led to the world market economy and the rise of capitalism. They sucked our blood and became fat. They built the new capitalist system on "the twin support of the slave trade from Africa to America and the piracy of American (Indian) silver."

And African people in these lands are still under the heel of oppression. After centuries in these lands look what is happening in Nova Scotia: racial riots. Blacks still denied access to jobs, schools, education and (can you imagine!) bars. The unemployment rate among African people in Nova Scotia is 80%. The racism in Quebec against Blacks is showing its vicious face: Francois Marcelus, a Black man killed by police on his way home from work; the police officer *thought* he resembled the suspect he was looking for. Haitian families being driven from a white Montreal neighbourhood because the whites do not want them there. In American cities we see African people dying from the vagaries of tenement urban living. All over Turtle Island we see white supremacy strengthening itself, being supported by governments and corporations. And all over the rest of the Americas we see and know that we are at the bottom of the pile. Did they bring us from Africa for this?

And who can forget Oka? In the summer of 1990 the world witnessed the Quebec police and the Canadian army trying to brutally repress the Mohawk people of Oka simply because they said you will not have anymore of our land. No, you will not pass. The Mohawk Indians defended their territory and the answer from the Quebec government was repression, repression, repression. Let's get rid of these dirty indians.

I am still defining my relationship with this land. I know I have to honour it, care for it and love it. I will mourn my

Arawak forebears. After all, they were the ones who took care and nourished the hills, mountain, valleys and rivers of Jamaica where I was born and so came to love. They first made music from them, made music to them, made love to them and took love from them. We know it was the Arawaks that first introduced cassava (manioc) cultivation and production to the rest of the world. They gave the canoe, the hammock and many other things to the rest of humanity. This essay is in honour of these people, the Arawaks of the Greater Antilles, with the hope that one day the legacy they left to us will be recognised and the brutal manner in which they became extinct will finally be made known.

The term 'Indian,' though not used much throughout this piece is used interchangeably with 'Native,' 'Aboriginal' and 'First Nation People.'

¹from the Holy Quran

Atabeyra

(Mater Dolorosa)

Atabeyra
Great Mother of the Arawaks
mistress of all moving waters
moon woman
lady of childbirth,
Night and day you drift on the foam
of the Caribbean sea
drifting from Florida to the Guianas
tearing your long hair
in grief for your lost children
Atabeyra
you stand on the tallest peak of Seville mountains*
straining your eyes over the vast expanse of
the Carib sea
looking for your lost children
Isis searching the world over for Osiris
Demeter mourning her loss of Persephone
Ishtar weeping for Tammuz
Yemaya lamenting for shango
Atabeyra
in your minds's eye you can see your children
making canoes
pounding dried cassava to make bread
playing ballgames
swimming
and shamans making sacred ceremonies

calling on your name
and the names of Yocahu and Opiyel-Guaobiran
and we know that when women want children,
a safe pregnancy and delivery they
invoke only your aid
Atabeyra
draw near
come, let me plait your hair
listen, though your children may be gone gone gone
to the overworld, to Coyaba
if you sit still and listen carefully
you will hear their voices in the wind and the waves
of the ocean
if you look intently you will see them walking swiftly
among the cassava patches
You should know Atabeyra that they are not dead
so please my lady weep no more

* *Mountains in Northern St. Ann, Jamaica*

MEMORIES HAVE TONGUE II

I think slavery is the next thing to hell.

HARRIET TUBMAN

Marie Joseph Angélique

Marie Joseph Angélique
hated the chains of slavery
she felt the strong should not oppress the weak
that all people should be free

She lived a slave in Montréal town
but in her heart she was free
so the city she did burn down
running for her liberty

But Marie was caught
and she was tried
and she was hanged
in the square of Montréal

Marie Joseph Angélique
did not want to be a slave
she preferred death to slavery
she preferred death to slavery
Oh freedom
oh freedon
oh freedom
oh freedom!

Harriet Shepherd

Harriet Shepherd, mother of five small children:
Anna Maria, Edwin, Eliza Jane, Mary Ann
and John Henry,
had had enough of slavery. So she seized her
master's carriages and horses and along with five
other slaves rode
to freedom
Maryland
Delaware
Philadelphia
Canada

Seven Children

Ann Maria Jackson lost her husband in the poorhouse.
He died, a madman, because two of his children
were sold
by massa
and even though in the eyes of Delaware law
he was a freeman
he still had no rights over his children

Ann Maria knew that more would be sold
Ann Maria knew that she had to be bold

So she took her seven remaining children
and lef massa
lef di plantation
lef di pain
lef di grief behind

In the Month of November, 1857
she arrived
with her seven children in St. Catharines, Canada
Free

Fleeing Girl of Fifteen in Male Attire

Maria Weems — aged 15
became a boy. Took the name of "Joe Wright"
and thru the help of 'friends' escaped to Canada
to Buxton.

Oh Canada

I

when she said she was going to canada
she never imagined it would be so cold
she arrived in the winter and as she stepped
outside the airport into the waiting car of her aunt
her nose began to bleed

II

tramping along parliament street
in snowboots that allowed water to enter
tramping to 'no frills'
where her aunt said you get the best bargains
along the street she noticed people, she later learnt
were called winos, scratching themselves
on parliament she noticed lots of West Indians
good sign, she thought

III

she never thought snow could fall so much
four days of it. a blizzard the girl on the tv announced.
people had to work in this weather, no you can't
stay home
her aunt said, or you will be fired.
one evening after coming home from work
her aunt told her that the wind almost blew her away
she had to hold on tight to a bus-stop

IV
sitting in the apartment all day
looking at the tv
shampoo to make girls' hair silky
tv stories with people who never seem happy
all my children
one life to live
as the world turns
when she saw a Black face, her eyes focussed
she paid attention

V
regent park reminded her of
tivoli
jungle
dunkirk
same square boxes with tiny tiny insides
in the stairwell they shit and piss on the floor
most times the elevators are out of order
in the park the boys play soccer
the girls watch
boys flirt with girls   dangerous love games

VI
two children with yellow hair
six and eight
they ask her questions
in your country do you live in trees
how did you know english

VII
the missis told her that her duties were
light housekeeping
but she was up from six o'clock to
whenever the family went to bed,
which was usually by midnight

VII
cooking
cleaning
washing
ironing
her weekend began saturday night and ended
sunday evening
at five, and this was every other weekend. spring.
time for spring cleaning
her missis told her to climb on the ladder
so she could reach the top windows. she said she was
not used to climbing, saw herself falling off
missis ask if back home she never use to climb trees

IX
she fed up
tired
angry
heartbroken
vex no rass
mad no hell
weekend off she never went back

X
her aunt not pleased
she said, you can't quit like that
rome wasn't built in a day
if you want good yuh nose haffi run
you haffi suck salt thru wooden spoon*

* *hard work is necessary in order to achieve what you want*

THE LEARNING TREE I

It's a hard road to travel
and a mighty long way to go

old spiritual

To Jamaican Women

To those women who rise
at five in the morning to prepare
food for their children and send them off to school
while their men lie
in bed

To those women who have no food to give
their children, cannot afford to send them to school
and whose men have disappeared

To those women who, in order to raise their children,
sweat inside oppressive factories
lie on cold sidewalks
hack an existence from rocky hillsides
take abuse from men who are their only source
of survival
this poem is for you

To those whores at Half-Way-Tree
with their mobile hotel rooms

To the young office girls who think
they hold they key of life in their hands

to those schoolgirls with their bright faces
whose dreams are sometimes betrayed by men
twice their age
to the unnamed
who by their unceasing work and action
cause life to flow unbroken

AFUA COOPER

To those daughters of Nanny
who are beginning to realise the power
they hold in their hands
This poem is for you

For Christine and Iselena

You did not want any particular honour

You did not choose the title "working mother"
it fell upon you as a matter of circumstance

You just wanted to live the way you wanted
and take care of your children
by using the best resources at hand

But this world was not made to accommodate you
you had to fight to get a job
and lose some of your dignity in the process
you had to battle arrogant men
in high and low places
you had to battle ancient prejudices
and
fight for daycare
fight for welfare
fight for the right to have and take care of your children
fight for the right to love whom you choose
And when you do these things
they dub you
superwoman
amazon
bitch

No you did not want any particular honour
you did not want any particular title
you just wanted to be

Aunts

Aunts sometimes are life-savers
they make sure they tell you things like the facts of life
bloody things like your period
and what to do when it comes
and what that means for your whole life
they tell you, that if you go with a boy
you can get pregnant
and some aunts will even tell you what to drink
to lessen the flow
Aunts sometimes are life-savers
I mean they tell you
carry yourself like a woman with integrity
go to school and learn so that when you become
a woman
you don't have to depend on nobody
not to sell yourself for 30 pieces of silver
not to put up with no good men
one aunt have told me
that she married such a man
she fell in love with his looks but he was in fact a beast
he abused her for many years
until one day she packed her bags
threw stones and eggs behind her (a sign meaning
she will not return)
and forever left the beast.
He came many times begging her to return
but for him her heart had turned to stone.
another aunt told me how she spent 20 years in
England and was ready to return home. She had
had enough of the cold of the climate and the people.

But her husband was not ready to return.
So she simply packed her bags and came home and
built a house in the sun.
aunts sometimes are life-savers
they provide themselves as role models for you
and tell you everyday that your life need not be as
hard as theirs have been.

More on Aunts

but aunts can also be quite unkind
they get upset when you disagree with them
they admonish you for your stubborn ways
they tell you no good will come of you
if you continue to follow your own way
they get uncomfortable when you speak your truth
they even throw you out
they can also make your life a living hell

The Sheep Poem

It's easy to become a sheep
because at every corner you turn
there stands a good shepherd preaching
his doctrine, surrounded by his flock

And if you say, no
I do not want to become a sheep
I'd rather be an octopus
a camel
a lioness/unicorn
a dove
or worse, a pig
then the shepherd and his flock will say
"oh you think you are better than us,
you are a boaster, you are so arrogant," or something
of that sort

Then if you decide to become a sheep
you find you still cannot follow blindly
the dictates of the shepherd
if you say to him as you jump over the fence
that there is a deep chasm beneath the fence
he will call you a liar and accuse you of insubordination

But to be a non-sheep means
you have to pay a dear price
you may lose your family
you may lose all your clothes and have to walk naked
roaming all the earth babbling
in a strange language that few understand

The Rich have Colonised the Trees

It is the trees that attract me. I am walking west along St. Clair Avenue and I look down Spadina Road and am caught by the splendour of the trees. So I turn south along Spadina road. It is difficult to pay attention to only the trees. I walk past big houses with equally big lawns. I realise I am the only pedestrian. Everyone whizzes by in cars. Two cyclists. Not so distant memories rise to my mind. Cherry Gardens, St. Andrew, Jamaica. I am walking on a road in Cherry Gardens, big houses, a solitary street. A doberman jumps over a low concrete fence and begins to chase me. I run, fear stopping the scream in my throat. His master stops him with a whistle.

Now on Spadina road, my pace has quickened, I breath faster. With periphal vision I look out for the inevitable doberman/german shepherd. The street is lined with beautiful trees of every description, the yards are also adorned with trees, tall and grand. But I am feeling resentful. "Why have the rich colonised all the beautiful trees?" And I think of downtown. *Blessed are the rich for they shall inherit trees, blessed are the poor for they shall inherit concrete.* I feel strange walking along this road. The same feeling as in Cherry Gardens many years ago on a similar solitary street. I think to myself that I do not belong here. I still half-expect the doberman to come rushing out at me from one of these *grandes maisons.* "Be calm child, be calm," I tell myself but even as I say that my pace accelerates. Casa Loma comes into view. I go to sit in the park beside it to calm myself.

When I die

When I die bury me
beneath tall trees
and please make sure I receive the sunlight

THE LEARNING TREE II

Bend me but not break me
put me in the fire but let me not burn to ashes
AFUA COOPER

Womanhood

We who were thrust out of dark caverns
into a maddening light
We who know no truth
        no honour
we who go through this madness called life
into the estate of adulthood
crossing no dividing line
experiencing no period of transition
having no celebration for our puberty
        our blood
No rites of passage
no lovesong
only a shameful quietude
an impatient sadness
Now here we hang — suspended
between madness, agony and absolute truth
becoming women
suddenly thrust into a sphere we do not understand
becoming women

The Black Madonna
(thinking of Jimi Hendrix)

All along the evolution
all along the untenable path
I search for my Black Madonna
but she refuses to show her face
I walk the earth like a nomad
I seek but cannot find
all along the path I trod (am I) losing my mind

All along the evolution
all along the untenable path
I search
for my Black Madonna
instead I find two unicorns
sharing the same set of horns
and a woman called Maria
who is a shaman, a healer
with them as my companions I search
for the promise locked between the portals.

Laverne

Laverne was the perfect one. Each time my mind goes to my childhood and to Laverne, I remember her as the perfect one. She lived with her grandmother on our street in Franklyn Town. Her hair was always well combed, she never talked 'bad,' spoke only standard english and her clothes were always clean. Laverne also never ran with us, or picked mangoes with us over at Franklyn commons. Sister Iris, her grandmother, made her world perfectly ordered. Once, when we were both eight years old Laverne came with her grandmother to visit my mother who was ill. She sat perfectly still on a small stool in the living room and never opened her mouth, never said a word. I watched her. "Come Laverne, come play," I said. Sister Iris replied for her. "Laverne does not play after six o' clock." Children do not keep time so I did not know or even care that it was after six.

When they were leaving, my mother congratulated Sister Iris on Laverne's good behaviour. "Such a well-behaved child," my mother said. Sister Iris mumbled something about "doing her best." But after they left my father stated: "Ah doan care what anyone seh, but no chile is supposed to be dat well-behave, a chile is a chile, it not natural, it not natural."

High school. Laverne was the model student. Her tunic the cleanest, her hair well done and though she was not very bright she studied hard and won the admiration of our teachers, plus she never got into trouble.

In our third year of high school a terrible rumour started and on the street tongues wagged. It was Darcel who knew everthing, confirmed for me that Laverne was indeed pregnant. It was too hard to believe. Too shocking. No, not Laverne. For she never looked at boys, much less *talked* to them, so how could she be pregnant?

Soon her shame began to show. Sister Iris took sick and had to be confined to her bed. But not before she threw Laverne out. No, not really. She arranged for Laverne to go live with a relative in distant Portland. How could Laverne, the grandaughter she had raised from she was a baby bring so much shame and disgrace on her, a Christian woman? She could not abide such an intolerable abomination under her roof.

That night, as Laverne stood with her lone suitcase and her bags under the street light waiting for the taxi to take her to Parade, from where she'd take the Portland mini-bus, I felt a great pity for her. Her belly bulged some and she slouched but as I looked at her I did not see her as she was. All I saw was an eight-year-old child sitting perfectly still on the stool in my mother's living room.

What's Left

All I have left from you
are the three pairs of gold earrings
three successive birthdays.

Six O'Clock

and he is having supper with his family
I can hear the children's voices
his voice, her voice quieting them
he plays the role of the devoted father
and -ah- husband
I cannot interrupt this family ritual
"I'll call you back," he says at the other end of the line

I am jealous of your wife and children
for the time you spend with them
while you see me only at intermissions

I berate myself
call myself a fool
want to put a stop to this, make an exit
but my flesh refuses to see what my mind sees clearly

Now he has stopped calling
but his silence speaks

I fight to break out of this windowless
room you have locked me in
somewhere in the tropics.

Sunset

Your face begs what I cannot give
you want my laughter, I give you tears
you want my joy, I give you sorrow
I have abandoned you, you say

We are standing at the doorway
and I do not want to leave
yet I do leave and hide my face.
You must not see me weep.
When our eyes meet they plead
for an embrace we dare not
share
Our silence is a pain we dare not
speak

Perhaps, there is still time for us
but there are dawns we must wake to alone
and not be afraid.
I leave you now
I always leave
yet I never leave you

How To Hold Your Man

Some of us were told when we were young girls
(directly and through osmosis), that if we did everything
right when we became women; that is
smile coyly
keep our legs sealed
never let men feel that we were smarter than they
learn how to cook
smile when we feel like crying
then maybe (if we were lucky) we could get a man
and be able to keep him.
But some of us were thinking beings and we thought
"surely we know women who did all these things and they
never got or kept their men and we saw within even our
own families, women who never adhered to the above bad
advice and they got men, were able to keep them and sometimes threw them out." And we kept on thinking and believ-
ing that the pulse of our souls and the beat of our hearts
would guide us through the land of danger and hypocrisy.
Because the advice given insulted us to our very core. It
was meant to stultify the spirit, kill the heart, shrivel the
body and destroy the soul. We rejected it. And became
women who did not know our place. Became women with
ringing laughter. Became women who knew that our ulti-
mate aim was to seek our truth and live it.

More Bad Advice

We were also told that a sore foot man is better
than having no man at all
that a one-foot-man is better than no man at all
that the worse kind of man is better than no man at all
so young girls and women put up
with dangerous men
abusive men who beat the hell out of them
stupid men
sickening men
because we were told that every woman needs a man
and that we are nothing without one
so some of us sold our pride, our self-worth
in order to get this dubious treasure
we were not taught to see the shining beauty of
our souls.

DANCING ON SKULLS

I want the bullet from his head
to make a Benin bronze
to make an explosion of thunder
to make a cyclone

JANE CORTEZ

The Power of Racism

The power of racism
the power of racism
the power of racism
is such that Neville who is six foot two and weights 210
could be threatened with assault by three white children

The power of racism
the power of racism
the power or racism
is such that a Yusef Hawkins was killed in Brooklyn
due to the colour of his skin

the power of racism
the power of racism
the power of racism is such
that the ROM* could mount an African exhibition
without consulting Black people

* *Royal Ontario Museum*

Founding Peoples
(for Canada's First Nations' Peoples)

In everything you read
books
newspapers
magazines
you read about the founding peoples
in everything you hear
tv
radio
intelligent conversations
you hear dem talking bout the founding peoples
and even feminists sometimes talk about
Canada's founding women

who are these founding people
and tell me, what did they find?
well I was told in school
they are the French
and the British
who came to this wild land and tamed it
yes, I was told in school
they are the British and French
who came to this wilderness and civilised it

when they came here
did they not see something
did they not see anyone
did they not find nations
and civilisations
and people who had been here since creation

did they not see the Huron
Iroquois
Mississaugas
Micmac
Ojibway
and Cree
did they not find people living on this land
living with it in harmony

these nations had no prisons
no jails
no policemen
because criminals were rare or unknown
these nations loved their children
did not abuse them
and women were the chief cornerstone
founding nations
founding peoples
but we know this land was not empty
it was filled with trees sometimes prairies
bears
deer
fish
birds
and people. yes people
who had already found, who had already found
who had already found this land

from the north pole
to the south pole
this land this *terre amerique*
contained people who had already known this land

and the whites came out of europe
out of their castles
out of their hovels
overcrowded cities
laden with diseases
some fleeing famines
some fleeing wars
some looking for adventure
new lands to conquer
in the name of god, the king and the queen
and the people they met were kind.

the Indians gave them food and shelter
taught them agriculture
sometimes they gave them their daughter
or it could be a sister
and tried to show them how to live
with the land

but jamaica people have a saying
"sorry fi mawgah dawg
mawgah dawg tun roun bite yuh" *
yes these people who came repaid their hosts
with robbery and
treachery and
a trail of broken treaties
they waged a war of destruction
upon this land
they raped the women
violated the children
killed or imprisoned the men
and hunted the Buffalo for sport

buffalo buffalo buffalo bill
how many buffalos did you kill

you massacre the buffalo
and you starve a nation
bring them to their knees
cause a bad situation

and every time I remember wounded knee I cry
and every time I remember infested blankets I rage
and every time I remember sitting bull I
shout FREEDOM!!!

and those from europe say
we bring you civilisation
we bring you god
we bring you the bible
we bring you religion
we bring you law and order
prisons
soldiers
policemen/rcmp
we so graciously bring you
smallpox
cholera
gonorrhea
tuberculosis
measles
alcohol

And they have befouled the land
polluted the oceans rivers and lakes

upsetting the ecosystem
but the Indians knew how to care for the land
they had lived with it for aeons
they said we don't own it
the Great spirit sent us to guard it
the land is our mother
and you never violate your mother
the land, you respect it

and today as politicians in Ottawa
fight each other
and the two so-called founding people wrestle
one another
everyone has conveniently forgotten
James Bay
Lubicon
Nitassiwam

and today as the nations rise again
and the prophecies of the wise ones
become manifest
we know who are the caretakers of this land
we know who are the real founding people
an respect due!

*you stretch your hand and give assistance to the needy
and they turn around and stab you in the back.*

My Piece

I want my piece
I want my piece
I want my piece

I should have gotten it in 1838
but did not
Now I want it for my people

we are the only people who came
to this part of the world involuntarily
we were the unwilling migrants, dragged here in chains
and when the chains were unlocked
from our necks, hands and feet
our masters were given twenty million pounds
as compensation for the loss of their property
but the property after centuries of enslavement
received nothing

In the U.S., Black ex-slaves were promised 40 acres
and a mule
what they received was near re-enslavement
thru sharecropping
lynching
the terror of the state and the klan

we are the only people who have worked so hard
for nothing
Reparations now!

Germany is still paying reparations to the Jews
the Canadian Japanese have waged a fight
for reparation
for the loss of their property, lives and dignity and won
the Chinese in Canada are claiming
repayment for the head tax that a racist government
imposed on them
And I am requesting my piece
I want it for my people

everytime you hear about Africa
it's always about how much money she owes
to the west
the world bank
the imf
and the other parasites
but can they ever repay Africa
for the plunder
the rape
the loss of human and natural resources

the little island I come from
the little island that the robber-admiral describes
as the "fairest land the eyes ever beheld"
is in debt
in great death
to the imf
the world bank
and other blood-suckers
but I say this little island owes nothing
can they ever repay us for the genocide
slavery and colonialism

We owe nothing
don't pay the debt and let the system crash

I want my piece
I want it for my people

I want to build a school
as a monument for Queen Cubah of Jamaica
who even though exiled
returned to her home island to rekindle
the flame of revolt
yes, I want to build a school as a monument
for Queen Cubah
so that children may remember her name

To build a hospital in memory of Mary Seacole
who cared for British soldiers in the Crimean war
but who died penniless

I want my piece
to make a movie about Nanny,
Paul Bogle, William Gordon and
the Morant Bay rebellion
to write a book about Marie Joseph Angelique
Black slave women who burnt down Montreal
in her bid for freedom

I want my piece
for those lost ancestors whose names I will never know
for great great grandma Alison
who left Africa as a slave but entered Jamaica
as an indentured servant

for my father who toiled 40 years
at West Indies Sugar Company and received
peanuts on retirement

Yes I want my piece of that 20 million pounds
to make poems
to make songs
to write books
to make films
to make art
to give to freedom-fighters

I want my piece
my piece
my piece
I want it for my people

I Don't Care If Your Nanny Was Black

I don't care if your nanny was Black
that you ate grits for breakfast every morning
that you knew a Black girl in high school
and she was nice
I don't care
because Howard Beach is dead
killed by white youths
who got off free even though witnesses
testified to their crime
I don't care if your nanny was Black because
six Black youths are in jail
charged with raping a white woman
and Donald Trump takes out a three-page-add
in the New York Times calling for their deaths
calling for the lynching of six Black youths
while the four white cops who raped Black woman
Tawana Brawley
are still on the street

so when you hear Black rage
feel Black anger
you raise your hands in exasperation and
white guilt pours from your mouth
and you start to tell the audience
that you are not a racist
because your nanny was Black
and you ate grits for breakfast every morning
and you knew a Black girl in high school
and she was nice
I don't care
you hear me I don't care

because for too long
we have held our pain in our very flesh
for too long we have held our wounded hearts
in our chests
for too long our eyes have seen
what we cannot bear to see
Our anger will rise like a red flood
and spread across this land
tear down monuments built on our blood
cast away false idols
and like Joshua, tear down the walls of this Jericho

Oh Canada II

Canada
of genocide you are accused
why is it your jails are filled with Black men
why is it your prisons are filled with Native men
what are your intentions Canada
that you seek to bound us so

Canada
of genocide you are accused
why is it 60% of Black children will not finish
high school
why is it that those who do are streamed into the
lower levels

Canada
of genocide you are accused
why is it your police officers
constantly shoot Black youths in the head and back
why is it your officers constantly rob Black mothers
of their sons and daughters?

South Africa

(Free Azania)
Written for South African Women's Day, 11 August.

How long does it take
how long will it take
what does it take
before freedom comes to those who seek it
fight for it
and die for it

South Africa
South Africa is on my mind
as visions of babies being shot and
pregnant women being attacked flash
across the screens of my mind
I see teenaged youth
with clenched fist
sticks in their hands
and rage in their hearts
trying to remove to tear apart
the foundations of apartheid

And workers march
workers strike
the women organise and mobilise
the women organise and mobilise
the forces, forces forces forces of victory
and capital is threatened
so Weinberger says
"We'll not allow another Iran,"
and so we know as we have known

that the seeds are sown
for war
and we accept the challenge

But my blood is frozen
and my guts spill out
as Azania goes through this long dark night
as she cries
I dry her tears
and give her my words from which to fashion
bullets!

A True Revolution

No Kamau
there won't be a revolution because people have grown
complacent, accepting, and no longer have ideals

No Kamau
there won't be a revolution
because once again they have brought in the colonisers
(americans) this time
to whip the people into submission

No Kamau
there won't be a revolution
because artists and other would-be revolutionaries
have lost themselves in the fantasy island of cocaine
and Ilie is no longer
Jah holy herb

No Kamau
there won't be a revolution
because the voice of protest is weak
and punanis rule the airwaves

No Kamau
there won't be a revolution
because gold chains shackle the necks and minds
of the people
while Black miners die in South Africa
Kamau
your name means (quiet) warrior
and we need warriors like you

to dance to the martial chant
we need Far-I
to sound Nyahbinghi drums
we need ones with the spirit of Nanny, Tacky and Plato
to plan and stategise
to lay in wait and strike
at the enemy knowing fully well who he is

We need, yes
for the people to cleanse themselves
to respect themsleves
to respect the female part of themselves
and to know
that woman degradation
Black woman degradation
Black people degradation
must stop.

we need for the people to realise love
for themselves and their neighbours
and to know that love indeed is divine
Then Kamau when all these and more tasks
are completed
we will have a true revolution.

CELEBRATIONS

Shout joyfully to the Lord, all the earth;
Break forth and sing for joy and sing praises.
Sing praises to the Lord with the lyre;
With the lyre and the sound of melody.
With trumpets and the sound of horn....

Let the sea roar and all it contains,
the world and those who dwell in it.
Let the rivers clap their hands;
Let the mountains sing together for joy....

Psalm 98

Old Woman I

When I am old I would like to have
my old woman friends around me
like Geraldine has now
they come and they greet her kissing both cheeks
they sit on the porch and eat things forbidden by
the doctor
and they laugh and chat in French
but it could be Swahili
English
Chinese

Old Women II

They still talk about the passing of their husbands
and sigh "it's better that way, he suffered much"
they all go to the hairstylists once a month
and all except for Josie, who says
she will see a priest
only at her funeral, go to mass once a week
They feel sorry for me because "young men today are
not like young men in our days,"
and they pretend not to brag about their grandchildren

I look at them and am not afraid of growing old.

To Khetiwe

So sista
you ask me
what can a woman who likes being big
a woman who likes her size
do when other sistas make unfavourable
comments about it
and coyly suggest weight-loss clinic
"It's not easy being a fat Black woman," you say

I can make a few suggestions
potential replies to throw back at these mawgah women
first tell them that you are into yourself
and because you are into yourself
you're not a slave of fashion
not a slave of Babylon
then tell them that thin might be in
but fat is no sin
next, ask if they know of their ancient traditions
that in southeastern Nigeria
the rich and not so rich used to send their daughters
to Old Calabar to make then beautiful
beautiful in this case meant
fat
plump
above size 12

Poetry in You
(for Akil)

You got poetry in you
you got poetry in you
you got poetry in you

you hear the drum playing
and you turn to tell me
quite seriously
that the drum is talking
that the drum is singing
and just as seriously you ask: does the drum
have a spirit
I smile to myself and think
you got poetry in you

You wake up and sniff the morning
you comment: it smells like a Jamaican morning
I ask what do you mean
and you say: the smell of the trees and the earth
yes little brother
you got poetry in you
you got poetry in you
you got poetry in you

Hajarah

Hajarah
I see you running
in the desert and hears wails of anguish rising
from your throat
as you seek water for yourself
but more so for your infant child

Hajarah
I see you running seven times
betweem the hills of Safa and Marwah
beating your breasts in despair
shouting to God for help
as your infant son lie on the sand dying
of thirst

But Hajarah
don't you know you are blessed?
don't you know you are not forgotten?
don't you know that soon the angel will come
and lead you to a place from which will spring
sweet sweet water?

And Hajarah
you will build a city
yes, around this well of sweet water
you will establish a holy city
and all the world will come to drink

Stepping To Da Muse/Sic

(for Bob Marley)

Bob
you make me move in an ancient way
in an ancient way that my feet never forgot
you make my feet, my body
do things I never thought was possible
you made me do old world dance
Dahomey dance
you make me the priestess
in a pure and sacred way
we don't need no more sorrow
and my body moves slowy, my arms uplifted
I am offering sacrifice to my ancient God

She Dance
(dream poem)

lawd look di way
    she dance
she dance
    she dance
she hold up har head
square har shoulders
all rigid-like
den she get loose
an start to shake
lawd look di way she dance
she dance
    she dance   she dance
      she dance
she dance

is like when she dance someting in har
like a dam burst open an start fi flow
an she jus dance dance dance dance
she dance wid di wind
fi di wind
against di wind
har hands held high in supplication to God
she dance and dance
now is like Damballah possess har
har body start rippling like a snake
undulating like the waves/seductive as the sea
(the woman of the ocean in har)
as she dance

99

dance
dance
      dance

but now har body contorting
she ben ovah inna pain
lawd she mus be dying
but look she come
to life again   and dance
and dance

chile is who fah pickney is you
who you belong to
who initiate you into di rites of voodoo
where you learn fi dance so
fi dance so
fi dance so

lawd look di way you dance

The Upper Room
(inspired by the singing of Mahalia Jackson)

Baptism of fire
baptism of fire
with your voice Mahalia
as you take me to the Upper Room to meet my Lord
Hallelujah!

You crown me with your chants
as we commune
as we converse with the holy spirit

You crown me with your chants
and I spin, yes
I stumble and then
I rise
my mouth opens and my tongue speaks in a language

Yes, baptism of chants
baptism with you voice Mahalia
as you take me to the Upper Room

Glossary

p.18. (My Father's Mother) Alienation from the land, high unemployment and urban poverty led many Jamaicans and other English speaking West Indians to seek work in the construction of the Panama canal in the early part of this century. Working conditions were harsh and the workers experienced severe racism. Many Jamaican families have at least one relation who went to Panama and never came back. Today, all over Panama are descendants of these early Black West Indians who went to build the canal.

p.19-20. (Memories Have Tongue) Frome refers to both the town and sugar estate in Westmoreland, Jamaica where in 1938, workers on the estate protested the deplorable living and working conditions. The colonial militia was called in to put down the demonstrations. They killed several people. The first outburst of nationalism came from these demonstrations that shook the whole island. Norman Manley and Alexander Bustamante were labour and political activists who sided with the workers. Both eventually became leaders of the country. It is important to note that the Jamaican demonstrations were symtomatic of what was happening all over the British colonial world.

p.23-25. (Roots and Branches) Cuba was also a place of migration. Many Jamaicans who went there, worked for multinationals like West Indies Fruit Company. Today the descendants of Jamaicans are to be found all over Cuba, especially in the eastern provinces.

p.27-28. (Christopher Columbus) Christopher Columbus, Genoese (Italian) sailor who, under the patronage of the Spanish crown, visited Jamaica in 1494. It is estimated that when Columbus and his crew came to the island there were about a half a million Arawak Indians living throughout the island. By the time of the British conquest in 1655 the Indian population had been totally decimated by forms of Spanish colonialism. Readings: Fred Olsen, *On the Trail of the Arawaks,* (Oklahoma 1974); Kirkpatrick Sale, *The Conquest of Paradise, Christopher Columbus and the Columbian Legacy,* (New York 1990).

p.29-34. (500 Years of Discovery) The Arawak Indians, sometimes called Tainos, were the original inhabitants of the Greater and Lesser antilles of the West Indies. Tradition and archeological evidence indicate that they migrated from Venezuela/Colombia but may originally have come from as far as Ecuador and Peru. They appeared in the Antilles about 2000 b.c. Columbus recorded in his diary that the Arawaks were "the best people in the world and above all the gentlest...." He was amazed at their kindness and hospitality. Ironically it was Columbus that initiated the demise of these people. The Arawak society was one without violence. They had no instruments of war and it was recorded by contemporary observers that they never fought even among themselves. Their culture was based on the production of Cassava but other crops such as the sweet potato, various squashes and beans were also grown. Sale notes that these were grown in a "multicrop harmony." Sale also notes that the Arawak system of agriculture seems to have provided "an exceptionally ecologically well-balanced and productive form of land use..." Not much labour was needed for food cultivation (three hours per week), and harvest was continuous. On Africans in America before Columbus, see Ivan Van Sertima, *They Came Before Columbus,* (New York 1976); Leo Weiner, *Africa and the Discovery of America,* (Philadelphia 1920); Abdullah Hakim Quick, *Deeper Roots: Muslims in the Caribbean Before Columbus to the Present,* (The Bahamas 1990); on Matthieu D'Coste, see *Dictionary of Canadian Biography,* vol. I, (Toronto 1966) 452.

p.39. (Marie Joseph Angelique) Contrary to popular belief there was slavery in Canada. The enslaved were Africans and Indians (commonly called 'Panis'). Both the French and British colonists kept slaves. Marie Joseph Angelique was an African Slave originally from the West Indies who in April 1734, on learning that she was to be sold set fire to her mistress' Montreal home in her bid to escape.

As a result over half of the city was burnt down. Marie was caught, thrown in prison, tortured and then hanged in the public square. Historians give her age as being 26, she was also the mother of twins. See Marcel Trudel, *L'esclavage au Canada Francais,* (Laval University Press, Quebec 1961); for a reading in English, William Riddell, "The Slave in Canada," *Journal of Negro History,* vol. 5 (1920) 261-377.

p.40-42. (Harriet Shephard, Seven Children, Fleeing Girl of Fifteen in Male Attire). These poems came about due to research done on the Underground Railroad, several stations of which terminated in Canada. Many women and children, while travelling on the Underground Railroad, faced great odds in their flight from American slavery. The majority of the rail users settled in the northen states but thousands came into Canada. See, William Stil, *The Underground Railroad,* (Philadelphia 1872); Benjamin Drew, *The Narratives of Fugitive Slaves in Canada,* (Boston 1856).

p.43-46. (Oh Canada) Regent Park is a low-income housing project in downtown Toronto. Tivoli, Jungle and Dunkirk are Jamaican counterparts of Regent Park.

p.49-50. (To Jamaican Women) Half-Way-Tree is a town in Jamaica, capital of St. Andrew parish. Nanny was the legendary African-Jamaican woman who was the leader of her people, the Portland Maroons. Not only was she a chief but a worker of the magical arts, military strategist and warrior. Nanny lived in the 18th century and led her people in many battles against the British slave owners and colonisers. Today Queen Nanny is honoured as one of Jamaica's national heroes. Mavis C. Campbell, *The Maroons of Jamaica,* 1655-1796, (New Jersey 1990); Lucille Mathurin, *The Rebel Woman in the British West Indies During Slavery,* (Kingston, Jamaica 1975).

p.62. (The Black Madonna) The Black Madonna is based on a dream I had many years ago. I did not know then that I was dealing with images and symbols of immense historical and archetypal proportions.

It was only many years after that I began to read about the phenomenon of Black virgins all over the world and what they represented. The original Madonna as we know it to be is the Black Egyptian Isis with her half-human half-divine son, Horus. This undoubtedly is the prototype of the virgin Mary and her son Jesus. I discovered too that the unicorn was a special animal of the virgin. Readings: Ivan Van Sertima, ed., *Black Women In Antiquity,* (New Jersey 1984), especially Part one which deals with "Ethiopian and Egyptian Queens and Goddesses;" Ean Beag, *The Cult of the Black Virgins,* (London, England 1985); China Galland, *Longing For Darkness, Tara and The Black Madonna,* (New York 1990).

p. 73. (The Power of Racism) In 1989 Yusef Hawkins was murdered by white youths in Brooklyn. His crime was that he was walking in a white neighbourhood. In 1990 the Royal Ontario Museum hosted an African exhibition. This was done without properly consulting members of the African community. This led to continuous demonstrations by members of this community. In one such demonstration the police were called in and subsequently eleven demonstrators were arrested.

p.74-78. (Founding Peoples) I wish to thank Lenore Keeshig-Tobias, Toronto based Ojibway writer and storyteller, for reading this poem for me and for her helpful comments and suggestions. Readings: *Sitting Bull;* William Wuttunee, *Ruffled Feathers: Indians in Canadian Society* (Calgary 1971); Kathleen Jamieson, *Indian Women and the Law in Canada: Citizens Minus* (Ottawa 1978); Jack Weatherford, Indian Givers; Jeffrey Goodman, *American Genesis, The American Indian and the Origins of Modern Man,* (New York 1981).

p. 79. (My Piece) In 1760 in Jamaica a plot of a planned insurrection was discovered. Prominent among the leaders of this failed insurrection was Queen Cubah, a Kingston slave. Several of the leaders were hanged but Queen Cubah was transported (sent into permanent exile). She secretly returned to Jamaica to plot another revolt but was again caught. This time she was hanged. See Lucille Mathurin, *The Rebel Woman,* 21; Michael Craton, *Testing the Chains, Resistance to Slavery in the British West Indies,* (New York 1982) 132, 360.

p.88-89. (A True Revolution) This poem is written in response to Edward Kamau Brathwaite's poem "SpringBlade," in his book *Black and Blue,* (Havana 1976). "Ilie" is marijuana and was/is seen by some groups of Rastafari as sacred and medicinal. "Punanis" refers to the female genitalia. In recent times a genre of reggae music has devoted itself solely to degrading and castigating women whose genitals have become the focus of negative wordplay. Tacky was a leader of a slave revolt in St. Mary during the 18th century and Plato led a slave rebellion in Westmoreland during the same century. *Testing the Chains,* 16, 127-139.

p.95. (To Khetiwe) Mawgah, Jamaican for meagre. Babylon, used here as a symbol of decadence and immorality. In one area of southeastern Nigeria slim girls were not considered attractive. So as part of their coming of age rites they were sent to Old Calabar, to fattening houses to put on weight. See Okokon Ndem, "Making Girls Beautiful in Old Calabar," in P. Zabala ed., *African Writing,* (London, England 1974) 82-83.

p.97. (Hajarah) Hajarah or Hagar was a Black Egyptian (Nubian) woman who was reputed to be a daughter of the reigning Pharoah. She was also the second wife of the Biblical/Quranic prophet Abraham. In Abraham's old age Hajarah bore him a son, Ismail, which aroused the jealousy of his first wife Sarah. Due to Sarah's anger Hajarah and her son were banished to the (Arabian) desert. They suffered from intense heat and when Hajarah believed they were at the point of death an angel (Gabriel) led them to water. The well was called 'Zamzam'. The area soon became a halt for caravans on account of the abundance and sweetness of the Zamzam water. The city of Beca, later called Mecca, was soon established around the Zamzam well. This city then literally grew up around Hajarah.

The annual pilgrimage that Muslims around the world make to Mecca is called "the Hajj" and this word is taken from the name of Hajarah. One of the rituals performed by each pilgrim is running seven times between the hills of Safa and Marwah "in commemoration of Hajar's anguish and faithfulness." The story of Hajarah and Ismail is partially recorded in the Bible, Genesis 16 and 21. See also Psalm 84; Martin Lings' *Muhammad, His Life Based On the Earliest Sources* (London 1983) pp. 1-3; Rafiq Bilal's *Egyptian Sacred Science In Islam* (San Francisco 1987) 37-40.

p.98. (Stepping To Da Muse/Sic) Bob refers to Robert Nesta Marley, Jamaican reggae superstar.

p.99-100. (She Dance) Damballah: Haitian/Dahomey snake deity of wisdom. The woman of the ocean refers to Yemaya, Yoruba goddess of the ocean, dreams, childbirth, fertility and secrets. Yemaya's original home is in Yorubaland but she has travelled to and lived in all the African communities in the New World.

p.101. (The Upper Room) Mahalia Jackson: famed Black American Gospel singer.